LITTLE
ENGINEERS

STEAM
PLAY & LEARN

BY ANA DZIENGEL

This library edition published in 2019 by Walter Foster Jr.,
an imprint of The Quarto Group
26391 Crown Valley Parkway, Suite 220, Mission Viejo, CA 92691, USA.

Distributed in the United States and Canada by
Lerner Publisher Services
241 First Avenue North
Minneapolis, MN 55401 U.S.A.
www.lernerbooks.com

First Library Edition

Library of Congress Cataloging-in-Publication Data

Names: Dziengel, Ana, author.
Title: STEAM play & learn : fun step-by-step preschool projects about
   science, technology, engineering, art, and math! / Ana Dziengel.
Other titles: Play & learn | STEAM play and learn | Play and learn
Description: First library edition. | Mission Viejo CA : Walter Foster Jr.,
   an imprint of the Quarto Group, 2019. | Series: Little engineers |
   Audience: Ages 5+ | Audience: K to grade 3.
Identifiers: LCCN 2018051105 | ISBN 9781942875772 (hardcover)
Subjects: LCSH: Science--Experiments--Juvenile literature. | Science
   projects--Juvenile literature. | Creative activities and seat
   work--Juvenile literature.
Classification: LCC Q164 .D9574 2019 | DDC 507.8--dc23 LC record available at
https://lccn.loc.gov/2018051105

Printed in USA
9 8 7 6 5 4 3 2 1

MIX
Paper from
responsible sources
FSC® C008080
www.fsc.org

Table of Contents

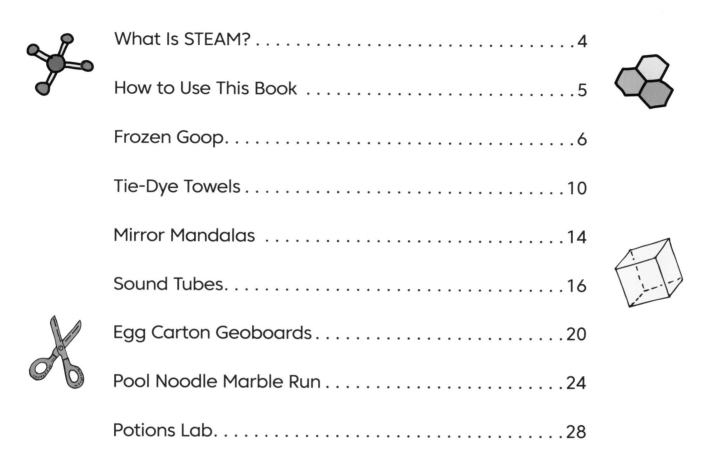

What Is STEAM?

The acronym STEAM stands for Science, Technology, Engineering, Art, and Math. STEAM learning is project-based and cross-disciplinary, with an emphasis on problem-solving and teamwork. Not only is STEAM a model for education, but it's also a way of approaching life.

At the preschool level, this doesn't mean trying to teach your kids robotics and engineering, but rather presenting them with open-ended projects that allow them to solve problems, make mistakes, get creative, and most of all, have fun. Page 32 has some more information about how you can best support your kids as they try the projects in this book.

How to Use This Book

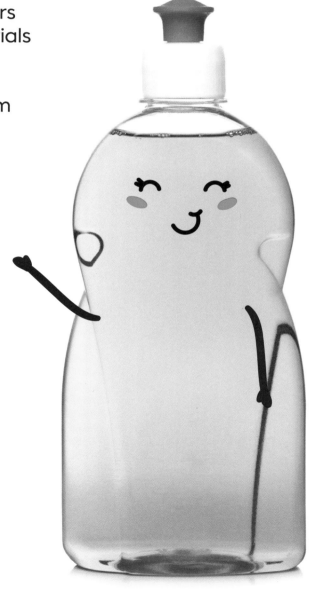

While most preschool children are not yet reading, this book is meant to be child-driven. The images, illustrations, and projects are meant to appeal to kids of their age and abilities. Let them be the guide as you explore the projects in this book.

These projects require parents and teachers to do nothing more than set out the materials and offer a challenge to children. A few of the projects will need parents to assemble components in advance of presenting them to kids.

> **!** Safety concerns are called out per project. Please read them in advance of working on a project. You know your child best. If they are prone to putting things in their mouth, skip the projects with marbles. Some project steps, such as hot gluing or cutting cardboard, should always be done by an adult.

Frozen Goop

A frozen substance usually has a shape and feels hard; a liquid is usually shapeless. In this experiment, you'll make something in between!

Materials

- Cornstarch or corn flour
- Food coloring
- Water
- Measuring cups
- Bowl and spoon for mixing
- Ice cube tray
- Tray or plastic plates
- Watercolor paper (optional)

Parent Prep

Fill the measuring cups with the proper amount of cornstarch and water.

1 Combine 1½ cups (192 g) cornstarch and ¾ cup (175 ml) water in a large bowl. Add food coloring and stir to combine.

2 Quickly pour the mixture into an ice cube tray.

Make different color mixes and pour into separate ice cube trays.

3 Freeze overnight.

4 Place the frozen goop ice cubes on a tray or plastic plate.

5 Play with the goop!

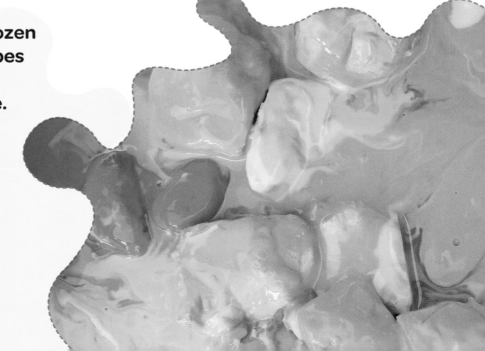

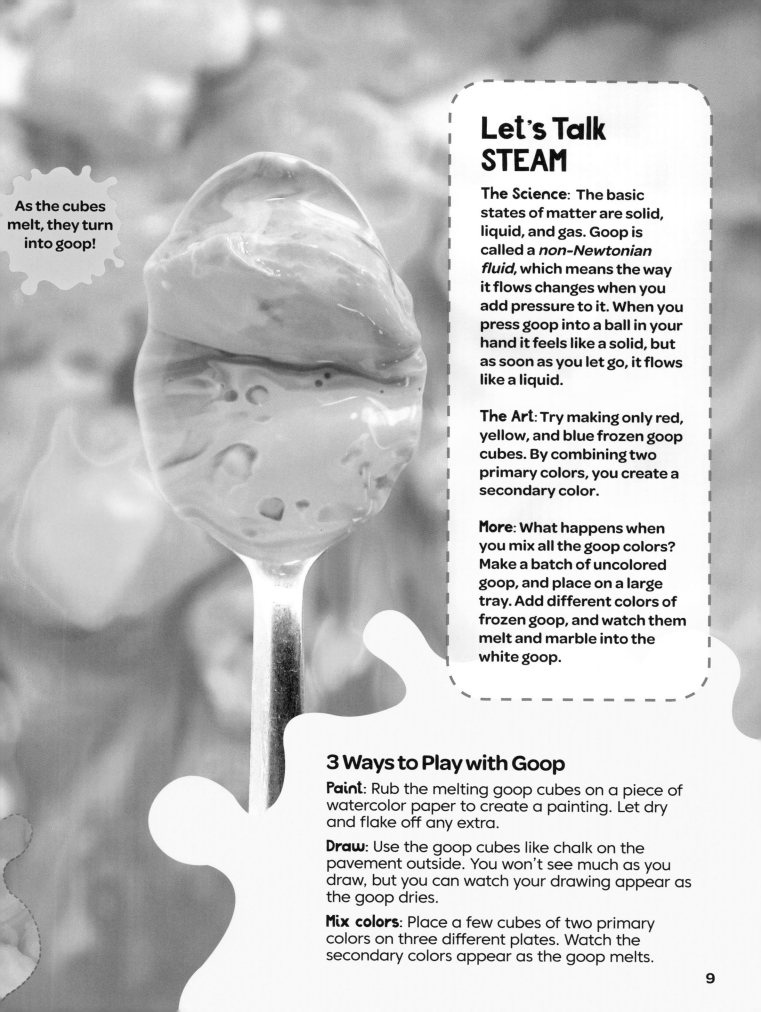

As the cubes melt, they turn into goop!

Let's Talk STEAM

The Science: The basic states of matter are solid, liquid, and gas. Goop is called a *non-Newtonian fluid*, which means the way it flows changes when you add pressure to it. When you press goop into a ball in your hand it feels like a solid, but as soon as you let go, it flows like a liquid.

The Art: Try making only red, yellow, and blue frozen goop cubes. By combining two primary colors, you create a secondary color.

More: What happens when you mix all the goop colors? Make a batch of uncolored goop, and place on a large tray. Add different colors of frozen goop, and watch them melt and marble into the white goop.

3 Ways to Play with Goop

Paint: Rub the melting goop cubes on a piece of watercolor paper to create a painting. Let dry and flake off any extra.

Draw: Use the goop cubes like chalk on the pavement outside. You won't see much as you draw, but you can watch your drawing appear as the goop dries.

Mix colors: Place a few cubes of two primary colors on three different plates. Watch the secondary colors appear as the goop melts.

Tie-Dye Towels

Ta-da! You'll feel like a magician when you unfold your brightly colored paper towels. But magic didn't make those symmetrical patterns—it was science, art, and math!

Use super absorbent, all-white paper towels.

Materials
- Paper towels
- Red, yellow, and blue food coloring
- Pipettes
- Water
- Jars or small plastic containers

Parent Prep

Mix the food coloring with water in three separate containers. The colors should be bold and not too thin or watery.

1 Fold a paper towel as small as you can. You can fold it into triangles, squares, or another shape.

The more times you fold the towel, the more patterns you will see when you unfold it!

2 Using a different pipette for each color, drip food coloring on one side of the folded towel.

3 Turn over the folded towel, and drip food coloring on the other side.

4 Unfold the paper towel to reveal your patterned design.

Let's Talk STEAM

The Science: Paper towels are made from trees. Trees absorb water through a process called *capillary action*. This is the ability of a liquid to flow upward and through materials with many little holes in them. As you drip colored water onto the paper towel, it quickly spreads out and through the porous material.

The Art: Red, blue, and yellow are primary colors. When they combine, a new color appears! This is called a *secondary color*. The secondary colors are green, orange, and violet.

The Math: Symmetry is when you see the same image repeated along a line called an *axis*. Each fold of the towel creates a new axis. When you drop color on these axes, you create symmetrical patterns, which you see when you unfold the towel.

More: How many different secondary colors can you make? What color appears when you combine the three primary colors?

> Make a bunch of dyed towels and tape them into a large quilt!

Mirror Mandalas

With mirrors, you can explore reflection and angles. Place colorful balls of modeling clay in front of two mirrors and see them reflected in cool ways.

You can buy mirrored sheets online or at craft stores.

Materials

- Small mirrors or mirrored acrylic sheets
- Duct tape
- Colorful modeling clay (homemade or store-bought)
- Paper
- Cardboard (optional)
- Washable markers (optional)

! Cover the mirrors' sharp corners with pieces of duct tape.

1 Place the mirror "book" on a flat surface with a white piece of paper underneath.

Parent Prep

Tape two small mirrors together like a book. If using acrylic sheets, first attach them to cardboard so they have a sturdy back.

How does making the mirrors' angle wider or narrower change the shape of your designs?

2 Roll small bits of modeling clay into different shapes.

3 Place the balls in front of the mirror to form a design.

Let's Talk STEAM

The Science: We see objects when light bounces off of them. When light hits a mirror, it bounces completely back and you see a reflection.

The Art: Mandalas are symbols created around a center point. Many artists use circular designs of color and objects in an eye-catching way. By using the properties of a reflection, you can make a complete mandala using only a few objects.

The Math: It's all about angles! When you place two mirrors at an angle to each other, light reflects back onto each mirror, and the image appears more than once. Change the angle of the mirrors to change how many reflections you see.

More: Try drawing on a piece of paper in front of the mirrors. Your design will be reflected multiple times to make a complete shape.

Sound Tubes

Before we had phones, we had a super-simple way to talk to someone over a distance: a voice pipe!

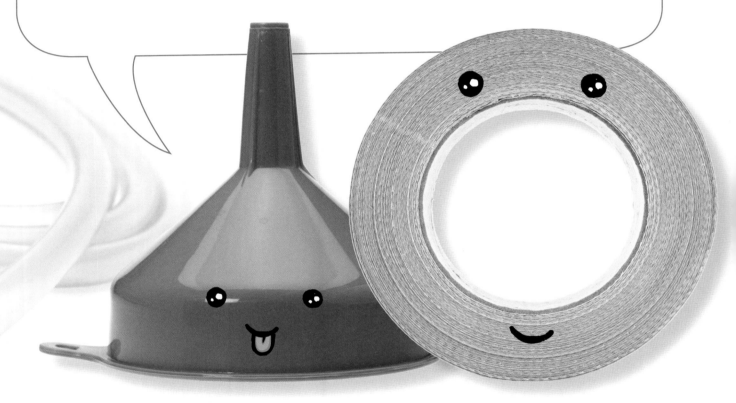

Materials

- 10 to 15 feet (3 to 4.6 m) of ½-inch (1.3 cm) diameter plastic tubing or larger (smaller tubing will not transmit sound)
- 2 plastic funnels
- Duct tape

The diameter of the funnel should match the inner diameter of the tubing.

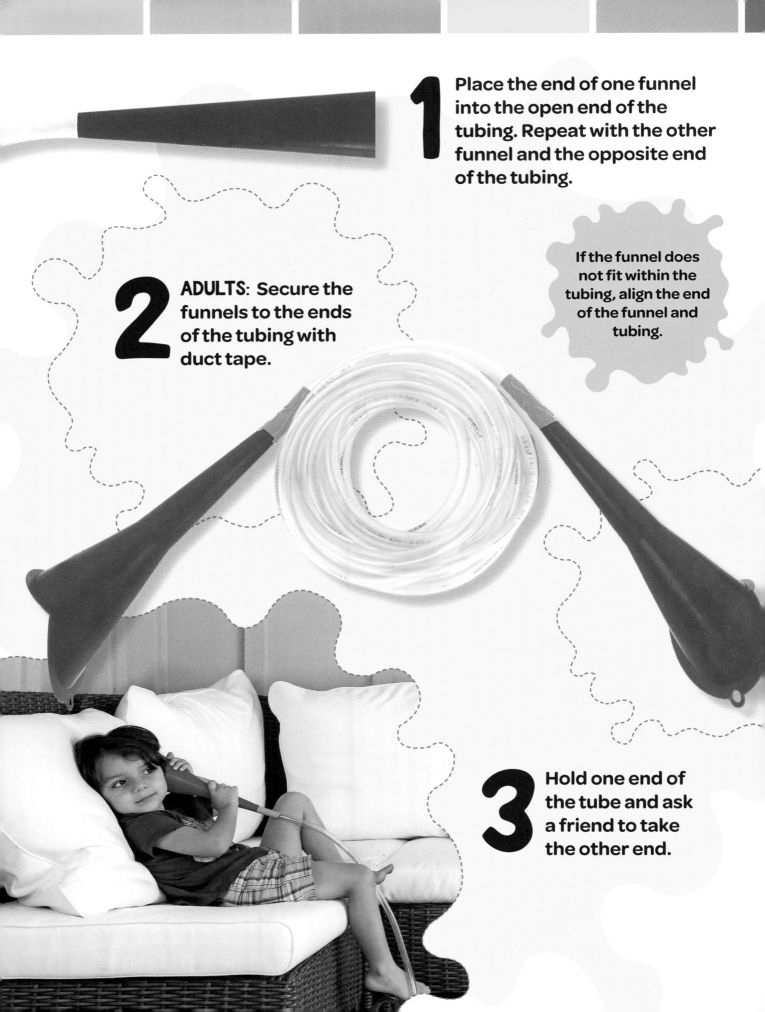

1 Place the end of one funnel into the open end of the tubing. Repeat with the other funnel and the opposite end of the tubing.

If the funnel does not fit within the tubing, align the end of the funnel and tubing.

2 ADULTS: Secure the funnels to the ends of the tubing with duct tape.

3 Hold one end of the tube and ask a friend to take the other end.

Be sure not to yell into the tube if someone's ear is on it!

4 One person should whisper into the tube while the other person holds the funnel up to his or her ear.

Let's Talk STEAM

The Science: When you speak, the sound of your voice travels through the air in waves. A voice tube concentrates the sound waves and blocks outside noise, allowing you to hear somebody from very far away.

The Technology: Before intercoms, people used to use a device called a voice pipe to speak to someone in the same building but in different rooms.

More: Blow through the tube! Does the person on the other end feel the breeze? Air movement can also travel through tubes! This is how a vacuum cleaner uses air to suck up dirt.

It will sound like the person speaking is right beside you!

Egg Carton Geoboards

Use stretchy rubber bands on this homemade geoboard to learn all about lines, shapes, and geometry! Can you create a cool picture?

Materials

- Plastic egg carton
- Large wood beads
- Rubber bands
- Hot glue gun and hot glue sticks (for adult use only)

! Large beads are a choking hazard. Supervise children carefully during this activity.

Parent Prep

Make the geoboard by hot gluing a large bead on the underside of each egg carton cell. Be generous with the glue to make sure the beads don't pop off when pulled by rubber bands. Let the glue dry completely.

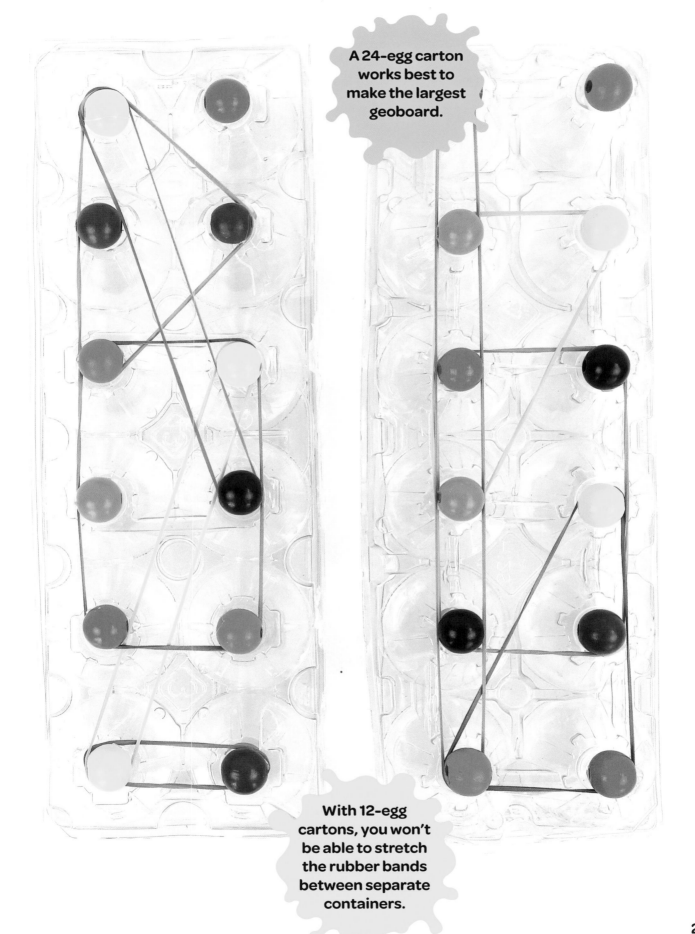

A 24-egg carton works best to make the largest geoboard.

With 12-egg cartons, you won't be able to stretch the rubber bands between separate containers.

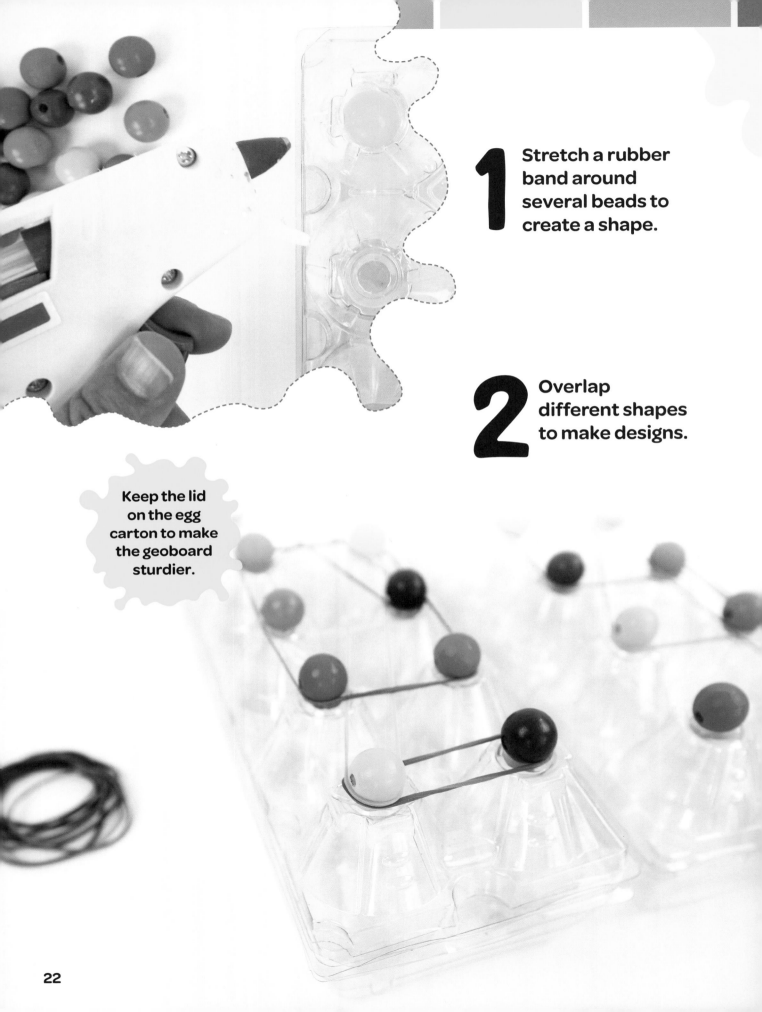

1 Stretch a rubber band around several beads to create a shape.

2 Overlap different shapes to make designs.

Keep the lid on the egg carton to make the geoboard sturdier.

Let's Talk STEAM

The Art: Artists and designers use many kinds of shapes. Some artists create art using geometric shapes, and others use organic shapes. Organic shapes are shapes that look more like nature, with curves and flowing lines.

The Math: Geometry is a type of math that studies points, lines, shapes, and angles. A shape is an area with an outline or border. Geometric shapes usually have straight connected sides, except, of course, for circles!

More: Can you make the basic geometric shapes on your geoboard: triangle, square, and rectangle? What other shapes can you make?

Try making letters! Can you spell your name?

Pool Noodle Marble Run

Create the perfect racetrack for all of your marbles. How far can you make them go?

Materials
- Pool noodles
- Marbles
- Duct tape
- Utility knife (for adult use only)

! Marbles are a choking hazard. Supervise children carefully during this activity.

Parent Prep

Parents, cut the noodles in half lengthwise with a utility knife.

1 Tape the ends of the pool noodle halves together using duct tape.

2 Repeat with several more noodles to make a long, continuous marble run.

3 Place one end of the pool noodle marble run over a couch, table, or chair.

Wheeeeee!

Let's Talk STEAM

The Science: *Velocity* is the speed of an object going in a certain direction. As the marbles roll down the pool noodle run, they may have too much velocity and pop off, or they may not have enough velocity and slow to a stop. The angle of the track will change how fast the marbles will travel down.

The Engineering: One of the most important things engineers do is problem-solve. As you place the pool noodle run on furniture and around the room, you will need to make adjustments to keep the marbles on the track and moving. What happens when the track is too steep or too flat? What if it is twisted? Will the marbles stay on?

More: Take it outside! Take your marble run and place it on a play structure. Parents can use zip ties to fasten the marble run to poles and fences. Get the neighborhood kids involved and see how long and far you can make marbles roll down a track!

4 Drop marbles down the run. Adjust as necessary so that the marbles stay on the track.

Tape helps keep the noodles in place on furniture or walls.

27

Potions Lab

Set up your very own kitchen laboratory! Use glitter and household liquids to create colorful chemical reactions.

Materials

- **Tray with sides**
- **Mason jar**
- **Vinegar**
- **Food coloring**
- **Dish soap**
- **Glitter**
- **Baking soda**
- **Spoons**
- **Lemon juice (optional)**
- **Powdered drink mix packets (optional)**

! Be careful! Lemon juice is a mild skin irritant.

Parent Prep

Set up the lab on a kitchen table or outside.

1 Place a mason jar in the middle of a tray, and fill it halfway with vinegar. Add some food coloring.

2 Add in a generous squeeze of dish soap.

The potion will bubble and foam over the top of the jar and spill onto the tray.

3 Sprinkle some glitter into the jar.

4 Add in a large spoonful of baking soda and stir well.

 5 Each time the reaction slows down, add more baking soda, vinegar, dish soap, glitter, and food coloring.

Try adding lemon juice and powdered drink mix to the mixture.

Let's Talk STEAM

The Science: When you mix baking soda and vinegar, a chemical reaction occurs. The reaction slows and the mixture becomes more foamy when you add soap. The citric acid in lemon juice and powdered drink mix reacts with baking soda in a similar type of chemical reaction.

The Art: As the different layers of the chemical reaction spill onto the tray, they form swirling patterns of food coloring and glitter. These patterns are another example of abstract art, which is art based on color and form.

More: What happens when you leave out the dish soap? Is the vinegar and baking soda reaction different than the lemon juice and baking soda reaction? Can you dip a piece of paper in the colored liquid to get a print? Can you take a picture of it?

A Letter to Parents and Teachers

No matter if you are an educator eager to incorporate STEAM projects into your curriculum or a parent who isn't sure what STEAM means, this book is meant to provide your children with a variety of projects that encourage them to be creative thinkers.

The projects in this book do the following:

- **Emphasize process**: The final product does not matter as much as the process of creating and exploring.

- **Encourage tinkering**: Kids should get comfortable making stuff and fooling around with materials.

- **Allow for mistakes**: Mistakes are the backbone of innovation. Kids need to learn to be comfortable with making mistakes and trying again.

- **Make connections**: Connections, particularly those between subjects, are all around us, and we need to foster them.

How can you best support children as they try projects in this book?

Back off their work! Breakthroughs often happen after a good challenge or failure. If your child is feeling stumped or frustrated, don't rush in with a solution. Instead ask them questions, encourage them to keep trying, or share a story of a challenge you faced and conquered.

Ask questions: When your child asks you a question, answer them with a question. Get your children into the habit of asking lots of questions and experimenting to find their own answers. This is the heart of STEAM-based learning.

Give them freedom: If you really want to raise an innovator, give them a lot of room to create. This means let them experiment, let them fail, and yes, let them make a huge mess.